Little Pebble™

Celebrate Spring
Rain Showers

by Kathryn Clay

CAPSTONE PRESS
a capstone imprint

Little Pebble is published by Capstone Press,
1710 Roe Crest Drive, North Mankato, Minnesota 56003
www.mycapstone.com

Library of Congress Cataloging-in-Publication Data
Library of Congress Cataloging-in-Publication data is on file with the Library of Congress.
ISBN 978-1-4914-8303-9 (library binding)
ISBN 978-1-4914-8307-7 (paperback)
ISBN 978-1-4914-8311-4 (ebook PDF)

Editorial Credits
Erika L. Shores, editor; Juliette Peters and Ashlee Suker, designers;
Svetlana Zhurkin, media researcher; Katy LaVigne, production specialist

Photo Credits
iStockphoto: dennisjim, 9; Shutterstock: Aspen Photo, 15, Brian A. Jackson, 5, Gayvoronskaya_Yana, 7, Geo Martinez, 20, georgemphoto, 11, Maksim Chaikou, 1, Marten_House, 19, Olha Ukhal, 3, Patrick Foto, cover, Photo Fun, 17, Stacey Ann Alberts, 21, tab62, 13, USBFCO, back cover and throughout

Printed in China.
007468LEOS16

Table of Contents

Spring Is Here!

Winter is over.

The days grow warmer.

Rainy spring weather is here.

Dark clouds roll in.

Lightning flashes.

Boom! Thunder bangs.

6

Tiny drops start to fall.

Heavy showers soak the ground.

8

Rain Helps Plants

Roots suck up the rain.

Stems poke from the dirt.

Leaves grow on the stems.

Flower buds grow.

Soon pink tulips bloom.

Rain Helps Animals

Rain makes puddles.

A thirsty deer takes a drink.

Worms die if they dry out.
Rain keeps their bodies wet.

After a Storm

Maya puts on boots.

She plays in the puddles.

The sun comes out.

Jackson sees a rainbow.

Glossary

bloom—to produce a flower

bud—part of a plant that turns into a leaf or flower

root—the part of a plant that attaches to the ground

stem—the main body of a plant

Read More

DeGezelle, Terri. *Exploring Spring*. Pebble Plus: Exploring the Seasons. North Mankato, Minn.: Capstone Press, 2012.

Fogliano, Julie. *And Then It's Spring*. New York: Roaring Brook Press, 2012.

Ghigna, Charles. *I See Spring*. I See. Mankato, Minn.: Picture Window Books, 2012.

Internet Sites

FactHound offers a safe, fun way to find Internet sites related to this book. All of the sites on FactHound have been researched by our staff.

Here's all you do:
Visit *www.facthound.com*
Type in this code: 9781491483039

Super-cool stuff!

Check out projects, games and lots more at
www.capstonekids.com

Index